MW01689275

You and Your Child's Teacher

Pamela Weinberg

SIGNAL HILL™
PUBLICATIONS

SIGNAL HILL™
PUBLICATIONS

ISBN 0-88336-627-4

Signal Hill Publications
An imprint of New Readers Press
U.S. publishing division of
Laubach Literacy International
Box 131, Syracuse, New York 13210

Printed in the United States of America

Illustrations: Bill Baylis

9 8 7 6 5

Table of Contents

Acknowledgments

Gratitude and thanks to:

my husband, Alan
my sons, Nathan and David
Lillie B. Stein
Melanie Freeland Taylor

Special thanks to:

Esther Zabitz
Myrna Rubenstein

To the reader

A teacher belongs in a school. So do children. As a parent, where do you fit in? Do parents have a place in the school?

As a parent, you can stand up for your child. You can make sure that he or she is getting a good education. Children need their parents to help them do well in school.

How can you help your child? How can you find out if the school is meeting your child's needs? How can you find out what is going on in the classroom? You can work with a teacher to answer these questions.

Teachers need your help, too. You know your child best. How can you and the teacher share ideas?

You and Your Child's Teacher will show you how to work with teachers. Open houses, conferences, and school fairs or plays are just a few ways. It's important to go to these events. The teacher will learn more about you and your child, too.

But these aren't the only ways to work with your child's teacher. This book will show you other ways to get involved in your child's education.

Chapter 1 will help you to contact teachers by telephone. Chapter 2 will help you to write notes and letters to teachers. In chapter 3, you'll get some ideas on meeting with teachers face-to-face. You'll learn how to get organized and keep important papers in chapter 4. Chapter 5 will give you some tips about being involved in your child's education.

The last chapter will show you ways to teach your child at home. You do not need costly books to help your child. You don't need a high school or college degree.

Remember, you are your child's first teacher. You are a key member of the teacher-child-parent team.

1 Making phone calls

Suppose you need to reach the school in an emergency. Maybe you need to take the baby to the doctor. You won't be home when your son gets out of school. He needs to know where to go until you get home. What can you do?

You can use the telephone. The telephone is a time-saver. You can use it to reach your child's school quickly.

Suppose your daughter brings home a paper with a low grade. You're not sure what the problem is. Or your son comes home upset every day after school. What can you do?

You can use the telephone. You can often work out problems with your child's teacher by phone. You can talk to the teacher and hear her side of the story.

Planning ahead

Be sure you know the school's phone number. Write it down. Keep it near the phone.

Before you call the teacher, think about why you are calling. What do you want to happen? Think about what you want to say. It helps if you write down a few notes.

Before you call, take out a piece of paper and a pencil. Ask yourself these questions:

- Who do I need to talk to today?
- Do I need to call right now, or can I wait?
- How do I expect this phone call to end?
- Am I calm enough to listen?
- What can the teacher do about the problem?
- Do I need to involve other people?
- What plan can the teacher and I work out?
- How can my child help to work this out?

Taking notes can help you spell out the reason for the phone call. When you plan ahead, you will feel more in control.

How to call

When you call the school, you may reach the operator first. Tell the operator the name of the school your child attends.

"Hello, this is Tracy Goodhart. Please connect me with Howard Day Elementary School."

The operator will connect you with the school. The secretary will answer. Tell the secretary who you are calling.

"Hello, this is Tracy Goodhart. I would like to speak with Bob's teacher. His teacher's name is Mr. Curry."

What if the teacher can't come to the phone? Ask the secretary to take a message. Leave your name, the name of your child, and your phone number.

"Please have Mr. Curry call me about Bob. My phone number is 555-1234. I'll be home after three."

What if it's hard to reach you by phone? Tell the secretary. Ask what time you can call the teacher. A good time to reach teachers is right before and after school. In most schools, teachers arrive before the students and leave after they do.

You might not be able to talk to the teacher. Ask the secretary if there is someone else you could talk to. There might be another person who works with your child.

It's important to talk to the teacher. But there are many other people in the school who can help you.

What if you're angry?

What if you call the teacher when you are upset? It's not a good idea to yell at the teacher on the phone. You may feel better after you yell. But the teacher won't. She might not want to help you. Stay calm on the phone. This will give you the best chance to help your child.

Staying calm isn't easy when you are upset. Think about what will work best for your child. Listen in on this phone call.

Mrs. Stoney (parent)

"My son, Blake, says that you pick on him. You people should know my son isn't a problem. You should do your job right and teach. Where do you get off talking to Blake that way?"

Mrs. Atmore (teacher)

"Listen, Mrs. Stoney, I don't know what you're talking about. Your son has been trouble since the

first day he came to class. He misses too much school. He has a bad attitude. He says he only has to listen to his mom—not an old teacher."

This phone call is not working. What if it started this way?

Mrs. Stoney (parent)

"I wanted to talk to you about how Blake is doing in school. He seemed upset today when he came home. Is there something I need to know?"

Mrs. Atmore (teacher)

"As a matter of fact, I've been meaning to call you. Blake and I had a rough week. He's not handing in his work, and his grades are dropping. When I gave him his paper today, he screamed out, 'This stinks!'"

Why does this sound better? This time, the parent talked about the child's feelings. Nobody accused anyone of doing something wrong. They both talked about the child, not about who is to blame.

Keep an open mind when you talk to the teacher. You want the phone call to go well. Avoid trying to say who was right and who was wrong. Try to smooth things out.

When you're on the phone, find out the facts. What really happened? Who was there? Is this the first time a conflict happened? Is there a pattern? Mrs. Stoney might find out that Blake is upset with school. She might also find out that Blake has some behavior problems.

Both parent and teacher should pay attention to the child. This will help them find ways to deal with the problem.

Still angry?

What if you feel the teacher is the root of the problem? The teacher works directly with your child. You should talk directly to the teacher.

Do not accuse the teacher of anything. Ask how you can help. Then listen carefully. Is the teacher willing to work with you? The teacher's tone of voice will tell you a lot.

Try to listen with an open mind. The teacher may be willing to make some changes.

What if you and the teacher can't work things out? Maybe you see the problem in different ways. Sometimes, the problem doesn't go away.

Try to work with the teacher first. But sometimes the problem can't be solved. Then you should speak to the principal or a guidance counselor.

Talk to another parent who knows this teacher. Talk to a friend and discuss how you see things. This will help clear your mind before you take the next step.

If you can't resolve a problem over the phone, you need to ask for a face-to-face meeting. Chapter 3 talks about ways to have a good meeting.

2 Sending notes and letters

Sometimes, a phone call is the best way to reach teachers. Notes and letters are good ways to communicate, too. In a note or letter to your child's teacher, you may need to:

- explain why your child was absent
- ask for the homework your child missed while he was sick
- ask to take your child out of school for a doctor's or dentist's appointment
- give permission for a class trip
- follow up on a phone call
- answer a note the teacher has written to you

Absence note

When your child misses school, the school needs to know why. You will need to write an absence note. Remember to include these key facts:

1. date
2. greeting
3. child's name
4. date of absence
5. reason for absence
6. closing
7. your signature

(1) May 3, 1990

(2) Dear Mr. Franklin:

My daughter, (3) Angela Cleary, was absent on (4) May 2 (5) because she had a fever and an earache.

(6) Sincerely,

(7) Donna Cleary

Practice writing your own note.

(1) ________________

(2) ________________:

(3) (4) (5) ______________________________

____

____

(6) ________________,

(7) ________________

Follow-up letter to a phone call

You and the teacher spoke on the phone last week. You haven't heard from her since then. You may want to write her a letter. Here is an example.

April 2, 1990

Dear Mrs. Rossner:

Thank you for your help. We talked last week about how Sara is not finishing her work. I talked with Sara. I am checking her papers. Can you let me know by Friday if you see any improvement? You can reach me at 555-1234.

Sincerely,
Cathy Spinner

Practice writing your own follow-up letter.

____

____________________:

____

____

____

____

____

____

____________________,

____

When there's a problem

Sometimes, a note has to deal with a more serious problem. This kind of note is harder to write. You need to separate your feelings from the facts.

Maybe your child is not improving in school. Nothing seems to help. You need to write about what you think can help him. The teacher needs to know that you're looking out for him.

Teachers like to get notes from parents. Notes show that you're interested. Remember, your child's teacher has a group of children to watch out for. Each child has needs. Notes help the teacher think about *your* child's needs.

3 Meeting face-to-face

Teachers have many children to think about. Your child is just one of them. You can help teachers focus on the needs of your child. A face-to-face meeting will help you. These meetings will help you and the teacher become partners in your child's education. They will help the teacher understand your child.

Does your child have a problem in school? Often, the best way to solve it is face-to-face. You can call the teacher, or write a note to arrange a meeting. Or you can wait until there is a parent-teacher conference.

Visiting the school

What are good times to visit your child's school? Here are some:

- open houses for parents
- workshops and classes
- parent support groups
- concerts or shows
- parent-and-child events
- conferences
- school projects
- planning for school events
- raising money for the school

Try to attend many school events. It will mean a lot to the teacher. It will also mean a lot to your child. When you come to school, you show that you care.

Meeting with the teacher

You may feel uneasy about meeting with teachers. You may not be sure of what to say. You may worry. A lot of parents have these feelings. These feelings will go away when you get to know the teacher. Here are some tips for meetings at school.

Be on time for conferences. This shows that you are reliable. Find out how long the meeting will last. Then you can plan to stay that long. Don't forget to ask to see your child's schoolwork. The teacher will be pleased you asked. Tell the teacher how you feel about things.

Sometimes it may be hard to say how you feel. Meeting with the teacher may not always be easy. What if you don't get along?

Let's take a look at this conference. Mrs. Weaver is meeting with Gary's teacher, Mr. Kohl.

Mrs. Weaver (parent)

"I'm here to talk to you about Gary. As I told his teacher last year, Gary is not slow."

Mr. Kohl (teacher)

"But Gary ***is*** *falling behind."*

Mrs. Weaver (parent)

"I told you, I don't like you calling Gary slow."

Mr. Kohl (teacher)

"Listen, I didn't say Gary was slow. He's lazy and he doesn't listen. He carries on in class. He's one of my worst students."

Mrs. Weaver (parent)

"As I understand it, you always pick on Gary. You give him a hard time. ***You're*** *the adult. You should know that Gary has feelings."*

Mr. Kohl (teacher)

"Feelings! Gary is rude and makes trouble. ***You*** *are an adult, Mrs. Weaver. I'd like you to keep your voice down."*

Mrs. Weaver (parent)

"I'm not your student. I came to talk about my boy, not get a lecture."

This meeting isn't going well. It's a shouting match. Do you think Mr. Kohl and Mrs. Weaver solved any problems?

How can Mr. Kohl and Mrs. Weaver get along better? What makes a good conference?

- Both parent and teacher listen calmly.
- Both people talk about the same thing.
- The parent isn't afraid to ask questions.
- The parent and teacher set goals for the child.
- The goals are reasonable.

Use these guidelines to rewrite the meeting between Mrs. Weaver and Mr. Kohl.

Mrs. Weaver (parent)

Mr. Kohl (teacher)

Mrs. Weaver (parent)

Don't say yes, don't say no

Sometimes, you may be asked to sign a paper. You may be asked to make a decision. But you haven't had time to think about it.

Why would you need to sign a paper? Maybe the teacher wants to put your child in a new program. Your child might need special education. Maybe the teacher wants someone else to test your child.

If your child needs special education, you must sign papers. Your child can't be placed in a program unless you say yes. When you sign a paper, you are saying yes.

Sometimes, you might not be ready to say yes or no. Sometimes, you need more time to make a decision. You don't always have to agree with what the teacher says. Keep an open mind. Think about what will be best for your child.

Remember, the teacher is looking out for both you and your child. But you have to live with your child at home. Decisions you make for your child will affect your whole family.

In many ways, your child has a lot in common with other children in the classroom. But your child will be different in some ways. He might need more help in school. Success in school might not be easy for him.

Don't make decisions until you are ready. Don't sign anything until you want to. Here are some things to think about:

- Do you have to make the decision right away?
- Is there a deadline for signing the paper?
- Is there someone who can help you? Can you speak to that person in private?
- Will your child get more services? Will your child get extra help? Who will pay for this help?

- Did someone explain any words that were new to you?
- Do you know how long the program will last? Can you see the program in action?
- Who is in charge of the program? Can you talk to this person?

How to follow up after a meeting

Here are some things to do after you meet with your child's teacher:

- Ask the teacher to send home a chart or paper that shows your child's progress.
- Mark the day of your meeting on a calendar. Call after three weeks if you do not hear from anyone.
- Ask for copies of tests and test results. Ask for a copy of any reports. These reports will go into your home file. (See chapter 4.)
- Write down what was said at the meeting. For example, "Mrs. Greenlea wants to keep Paula in third grade for another year."
- Write down how you feel. For example, "I am not sure what to do."

It is not easy to make decisions. Trust your feelings. You know your child best. Don't let other people make decisions for you. Find out what the school has done to help your child. Ask if there are other options that might help your child.

Don't say no too quickly. Your child may need extra help. Your child may need to learn in a different classroom.

Sometimes it helps if you talk to your friends. They may have made the same decisions with their children. They may know how you feel.

Remember, think about what is best for your child. As a parent, you'll have to make many decisions. Meeting face-to-face with teachers can sometimes make your decisions easier.

PTO MEETING
SCHOOL LUNCH MENU
REPORT CARD
FIELD TR
HEALTH RECORD
ASSEMBLY

4 Keeping a home file

Have you ever lost something you needed? No matter how hard you try, you can't remember where you put it.

This happens to parents all the time. When your child is in school, many papers come into your house. Which papers should you keep? Which should you throw away? Which papers are important? Which papers will you need later?

One way to keep track of important papers is to make a home file. A home file helps you:

- keep all your papers in one place
- keep papers organized for meetings
- save copies of important papers to refer to at a later date
- keep track of your child's progress

Important papers for your home file

Buy a file folder for each of your children. You might need a new one for each grade. File folders can be found in discount stores and drugstores. They cost less than one dollar. Look in the office or school sections.

Inside the file folder, place school papers you need to save. You can keep your file in a plastic letter file box, in a plastic basket, or in a desk drawer.

Some important papers you should keep in this file are:

- medical reports
- report cards
- school reports
- eyeglass prescriptions
- phone numbers
- letters to and from teachers
- Individual Educational Programs (IEPs)
- copies of papers you have signed (When you are asked to sign a paper at school, ask for a copy. Place the copy in your home file.)

Try something new

You can keep a diary of what goes on at your child's school. Use any kind of notebook for your diary. Keep it with your home file.

Start the diary on the first day of school. Write a few lines about how you feel. Include pictures of your child. You can also include pictures of projects he or she made for school. Look at this example.

Monday

I called school today. I talked to Jon's homeroom teacher. I told her Jon forgot his lunch money.

Tuesday

Today was report card day. Jon had a "D" in reading. Last time he had a "B." I was upset. I felt better after I talked to my sister Rose.

Wednesday

I talked to Jon's reading teacher. She said he forgot to turn in a book report worth 100 points. That's why he got a "D" this time.

Thursday

My sister took Jon to the library. He won't miss turning in this month's book report.

Friday

Jon won first prize in a math contest.

It's hard to keep track of your child's progress in school. Home files and diaries can help. A home file will keep important papers organized. A diary will help you and your child see day-to-day progress.

5 How to work with teachers

Here are 26 tips that will help you work with teachers. All of them will help you to be a partner in your child's education.

A Be **alert** to signs that your child needs help.

B **Build** a **bridge** from home to school.

C **Communicate** with your child and his teacher.

D **Discuss** everything.

E Ask the teacher to **explain** things clearly.

F **Follow up** after meetings or phone calls.

G **Go** to open houses or parent programs at school.

H **Help** your child at **home**.

I Be **involved** and **interested** in your child's school.

J **Join** with other parents and share ideas.

K **Know** your rights as a parent.

L Write a thank-you **letter** to a helpful teacher.

M **Meet** the teacher face-to-face.

N **Notice** the good things your child does—at home and at school.

O **Open** your mind to new ideas.

P **Prepare** your child for school by teaching him at home.

Q Ask **questions.** Speak up if you don't understand something.

R **Read** school notes. If you have trouble reading them, ask for help.

S **Search** for new ways to help your child learn at home.

T Use the **telephone** to communicate with your child's teacher.

U **Understand** your child's needs.

V Stay **visible** so people at school will get to know you.

W Don't **wait** for your child to have a problem in school before you talk to her teacher.

X Get **eXcited** when your child shows success.

Y Remember, **you** are your child's teacher, too.

Z Don't just **zip** in and out of school.

6 Home learning activities

Being a partner in your child's education means a lot of things. It means talking and working with teachers. But school is not the only place where children learn.

Your child learns many things from you at home. When parents are teachers at home, the home-school link becomes stronger.

Don't worry if you don't have a lot of time to spend with your child. Every little bit counts. Your child needs to spend some time alone with you. There are many things you can do.

One-to-one time

One-to-one time shows your child how much you care. It shows your child that learning is important—at home and at school. There are many things you can do during one-to-one time.

You can take your child to the store. Or for a walk. Talk together. This will teach your child a lot of new words. Talk about the weather, the traffic, or even people passing by. The more she hears, the more she will learn.

One-to-one time can be spent reading or looking at a book, doing jobs around the house, watching TV in the same room, or just talking.

One-to-one time may not seem very important. But it means everything to your child.

Homework helpers

What if your child wants help with homework? This is one-to-one time, too.

Can you find a corner or spot in your house where your child can work quietly? Do you have a box or other place to keep school supplies? Many parents think they need to buy workbooks and costly learning aids. These things aren't important. You don't need them to help your child learn at home.

You probably have some school supplies in your home. You may need to buy only a few things. To do homework, your child will need pencils, a pencil sharpener, crayons, and paper—both lined and unlined. It's a good idea to keep the school supplies in one place.

Homework reviews what your child learned at school. But sometimes he might not be sure about how to do the work. What can you do to help?

Remember, you are your child's first teacher. Helping with homework is important. Before you help your child, make sure he tries the work alone. Then you can work together. You can set up a daily homework time. And make sure there's a good place for you both to work.

What if it's hard for you to help your child? Maybe a friend can help you. Or you can ask the teacher for help.

Helping with homework is important. But there are other ways to help your child learn, too. Learning doesn't have to come from a book or a piece of paper. Does your child like to collect things? Does your child like to look at pictures? There are many ways to help your child learn.

Picture box

A picture box can help children of all ages. It's a box to store all kinds of pictures. Preschoolers and teenagers can use pictures for learning games. Pictures can be used for math, social studies, science, and language arts.

Making a picture box is fun and easy. You'll need an empty box. A shoe box is good, but any size box will work. Your child may want to draw and color on the outside of the box. Keep the picture box near the school supplies.

You don't have to buy pictures to put in the box. Save colorful ads and magazines. Save old newspapers. Save greeting cards and postcards.

Put markers, crayons, pencils, glue or tape, and a pair of scissors in your box. (Remember not to let a young child use scissors without you.) You'll need plain paper or construction paper, too. Keep the paper on a shelf near the box.

Here are a few ways to use the pictures in your picture box:

Greeting cards

Make a homemade card. Fold a piece of paper in half. Paste a picture on the outside of the paper. Write a message inside.

Book report covers

Does your child have to hand in a book report? Look through the picture box. Find a picture for the front cover of the report.

A-B-C book

Look through the pictures. Pick a picture that stands for each letter of the alphabet. Make a book with one letter and one picture on each page.

"Do you see what I see?"

Take a picture that has many things in it. Ask your child if he sees the things you describe. For example, "In this picture, do you see people laughing?"

Puppet show

Find pictures of people. Glue them on popsicle sticks. You and your child can make up stories for a puppet show.

Tell a story

Have your child choose a picture and then tell a story about it.

Picnic basket

Draw a picnic basket on a sheet of paper. Paste in pictures of all the foods and drinks you would take on a picnic.

"If I had a dollar..."

How much do things cost? Make two columns on a piece of paper. At the top of one column write "one dollar or less." At the top of the other write "five dollars or less." Look through the food ads and find out how much food costs. Paste pictures of food in the right price column.

Wrap-up

Paste pictures from the comics on tissue paper. Use the tissue paper to wrap presents.

Opposites

Fold a sheet of paper in half. On one side of the paper, paste a picture. On the other side, paste a picture that is the opposite of the first one. For example, a picture of a summer scene is the opposite of a winter scene.

Coupons

Look at pictures on coupons. Ask your child if you have any of those products in your house.

Things that grow

Have your child find pictures of things that grow. Paste them on a sheet of paper.

Famous people

Find pictures of famous people. Paste them on a sheet of paper. Under the picture, write, or have your child write, the people's names and why they are famous.

Go-togethers

Help your child match up pictures that are related. For example, cup-saucer; hammer-nail; mother-baby.

"Tell me why (who, what, where, when)"

Play a game of asking questions about the pictures. Take turns asking questions like, "Why do the men have hats on?" or, "Where is the little boy going?"

Final thoughts

Helping your child with school may seem hard at times. And notes from teachers are sometimes hard to understand. A lot of parents have these feelings. But it's important to know that you *can* help your child.

You can help by sending your child to school every day. Your child's teacher has prepared a lesson for each day. If your child is not in school, he will miss the lesson. Each day he misses makes it harder and harder for him to catch up.

You can help by communicating often with the teacher. The teacher wants to hear from you. Meeting face-to-face and talking on the phone are important.

Being involved makes a difference. Your child's teacher is trained to help your child learn. That doesn't mean she can do the job alone. She needs your help. Parents, children, and teachers need to work together to make a child's education the best.